Wake up to the World of Science

SOUND AND NOISE

Burke Publishing Company Limited

LONDON   TORONTO   NEW YORK

First published in the English language 1988
© Burke Publishing Company Limited 1988
Translated and adapted from *Les bruits et les sons* by Merigot, Escleyne and Schrab
© Editions Fernand Nathan 1985

Acknowledgements
The publishers are grateful to Jennifer Dyke for preparing the text of this edition and to the following for permission to reproduce copyright illustrations:
    Charmet; Gamma/Bramly; Hewett Street Studios/Chris Christodoulou, Massiot-Philips; Philips; Rapho/Rouget; Sygma/Schachmes.

CIP data
Merigot, M.
    Noise and Sound.
    I. Sound – For children 2. Noise – For children
    I. Title II. Escleyne, G. III. Schrab, D.
    IV. Series
534

ISBN 0 222 01079 7 Hardbound
ISBN 0 222 01080 0 Paperback

Burke Publishing Company Limited
Pegasus House, 116-120 Golden Lane, London EC1Y 0TL, England.
Burke Publishing (Canada) Limited
Registered Office: 20 Queen Street West, Suite 3000, Box 30, Toronto, Canada M5H 1V5.
Burke Publishing Company Inc.
Registered Office: 333 State Street, PO Box 1740, Bridgeport, Connecticut 06601, U.S.A.
Filmset in Souvenir by Trendsetters, Hull, England.
Printed in Spain by Graficas Reunidas

Contents

Seeing and hearing

I can hear voices. A gleam of light in my eyes.
The bells are ringing in St Peter's church.
Bathers calling: "Come closer! Move back! Over here!
No, over there!" Birds are twittering. Jeanne twitters too.
George calls to her. Cocks crow. A trowel
Scraping on a roof. Horses trotting down the lane.
The swish of a scythe through the grass.
Bangs, thuds . . .

Victor Hugo: *On being a grandfather*

What do you hear?
– What sort of noises do you like?
  And which don't you like?
– Are there any noises which send you to sleep?
  Any which make you happy or afraid?

Harmonious sounds

Noises

"Pleasant" sounds, in which you can distinguish different notes.

Jumbled, discordant sounds which the ear finds totally unmusical.

Find examples of different noises and sounds.

Something to do: Make noises with various things – such as glasses, keys or metal objects – and try to imitate the sound with your voice or a musical instrument.

Vibration of the vocal cords

The human voice
Put a piece of thin paper on your lip; as you speak you will feel vibrations.

Something to do: Make a tom-tom.
Take a round box without a lid, and stretch a thin skin or membrane over the top (part of a balloon would be ideal), secured with an elastic band.

Put a small amount of sand on the membrane. When you tap the membrane it will vibrate and make sounds. At the same time, you will see the grains of sand jumping up and down.

Think: What will happen if you put your hand on the membrane for a long time?

Vibration of other things

The tuning fork

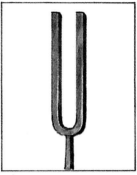

Make it vibrate by striking one of the branches against a table.
Put it to your ear. What do you hear?
Put it to your lips. What do you feel?

Another instrument for you to make:
Make two holes in a cardboard roll as shown. Close the ends with some very thin paper (tissue paper) and secure the paper with a piece of thread or an elastic band. As you blow down the holes the paper over the ends vibrates and makes a sound.

Think: What will happen if you hold one end of a ruler firmly on the edge of a table and press down on the other end? Why?

To produce sounds, we must make things vibrate.

Making sounds with your voice

When you talk or shout, air is forced out of your lungs, making the vocal cords vibrate and produce sounds; your mouth, tongue and teeth modify these sounds.

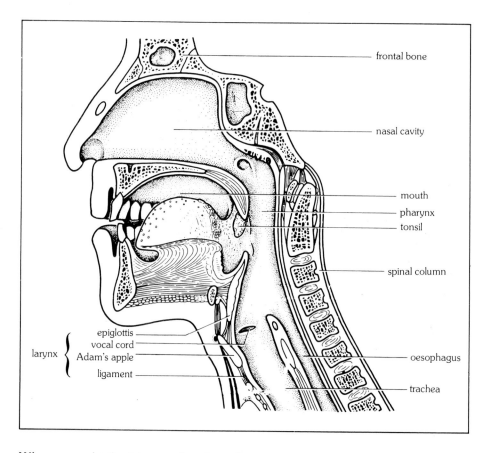

When you whistle, it is your lips that vibrate.

When they speak, human beings are capable of making about fifty different sounds.

There are between 2,500 and 3,500 languages in the world, each with its own sounds.

There are many sounds we can make with our voice besides those in our own language.

The vocal cords and the lips produce sound when they vibrate.

High sounds and low sounds

Be a singer

Sing a low note, then sing the same note a bit higher, and then higher again. It seems as though the low note comes from low down in your body, whereas you must stand tall and stretch up to produce the higher notes.

That is probably why we talk about "high" notes.

Opera-singers have different names according to their vocal register.

Something to do: Look up the meaning of these words for vocal registers in the glossary on page 32:

    bass
    baritone
    tenor
    soprano

with musical instruments

A flautist makes the air move with his lips, so does a recorder-player. But an oboe has a double reed which vibrates to produce a sound.

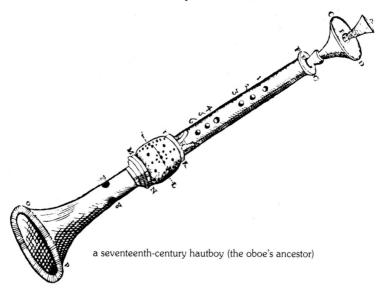

a seventeenth-century hautboy (the oboe's ancestor)

Anything which vibrates can produce a sound

plucking　　　　　**striking**

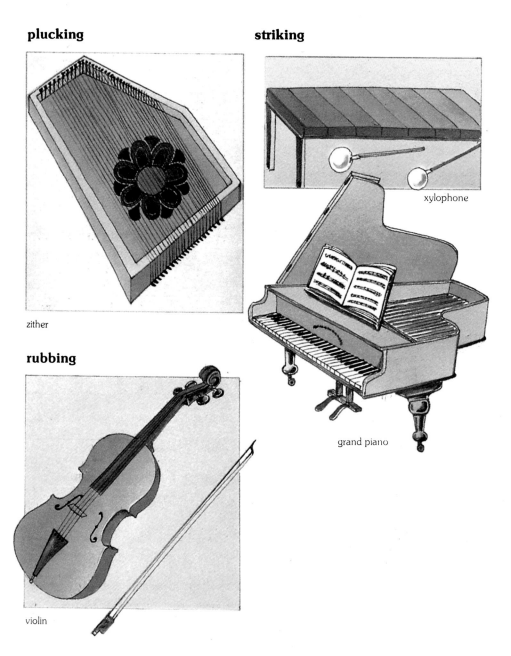

zither

xylophone

rubbing

grand piano

violin

The violin, the cello and the double bass belong to the same family: the way in which the vibrations are made is exactly the same, yet the sounds produced are different. The strings make the notes, but the sound box modifies and amplifies the sound produced.

Things to do:
1. Pluck, rub or strike various objects. Are you making a sound?
2. Notice that the different objects vibrate.
3. Think of other families of instruments, and explain what makes the sound.

We make sounds by causing something to vibrate.

All about strings

Look at this harp. It plays different notes because the strings are of different lengths.

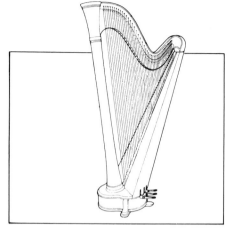

Something to do:
Ask a grown-up to help you make a small harp with a piece of wood, a few nails and wire or elastic. But mind your fingers!
Use different materials for the strings (wire, elastic . .) and compare the sounds they make.

If you replace the strings with metal plates of varying lengths, you get a xylophone.

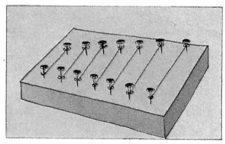

A familiar stringed instrument:

the guitar
The strings are of different thicknesses (1). The pegs (2) tighten or loosen the strings to enable you to tune the instrument.

When you play the guitar, you change the length of the strings by pressing them against the frets with your fingers or a capo (3).

The shorter and tighter a string is, the higher the note it makes.

Making other instruments

Using flower pots

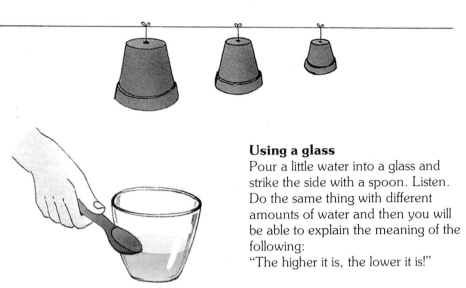

Using a glass
Pour a little water into a glass and strike the side with a spoon. Listen. Do the same thing with different amounts of water and then you will be able to explain the meaning of the following:
"The higher it is, the lower it is!"

A bottle orchestra

Choose eight identical bottles. Carefully adjust the amount of water in each so as to make a scale. Then play this tune with your bottle ensemble.
Describe what happens.

You can see that the highest notes are produced with the lowest level of water.

How sounds travel through the air

To help you understand

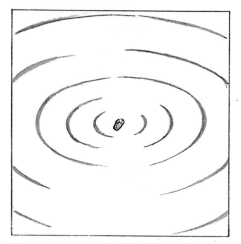

Have you noticed what happens when you throw a stone into the water? It is as if the stone were pushing the water away. A circle forms which gets bigger and bigger – followed by more circles.

When a balloon bursts, something very similar happens.
The sound-waves spread through the air in an ever-widening circle.

The further they travel, the weaker the sound-waves become. The farm-workers on the extreme left of the picture below hear the church bell more faintly than the two men in the foreground.

Air transmits sounds.

How sounds travel through other materials

Solid materials conduct sound very well.

On the moon

The moon has no atmosphere: silence reigns.
Sound needs something through which to travel.

Sound travels through:
- the air at 340 metres (1,115 feet) per second
- water at 1,500 metres (4,921 feet) per second
- steel at 5,100 metres (16,732 feet) per second

Calculate the distance sound travels in one minute through these different materials.

All materials will transmit sound to some extent.
But sound cannot travel through a vacuum.

The speed of sound and the speed of light

The speed of light through the air is 300,000 kilometres (186,420 miles) per second. Compare this with the speed of sound.

An experiment

balloon

look carefully
listen carefully

POP!

Go to an open space and stand a good distance away from a grown-up holding a balloon with instructions to burst it with a sharp pin.

If you are far enough apart, you will see the balloon burst before you hear the bang.

A thunderstorm

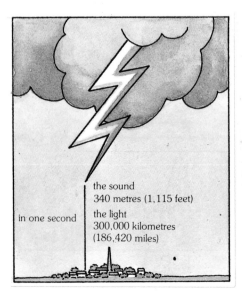

the sound
340 metres (1,115 feet)

in one second

the light
300,000 kilometres
(186,420 miles)

The time lapse between seeing and hearing the same thing.

During a thunderstorm you see the lightning long before you hear the thunder. The picture alongside will help you understand this well-known rule: "To find out the distance (in metres) between you and the thunderbolt, multiply the number of seconds between seeing the lightning and hearing the thunder by 340." (The distance in kilometres is found by dividing the number of seconds by 3).

Light and sound travel at different speeds.

A perfect sound receiver: the ear

Look at this drawing of the human ear:

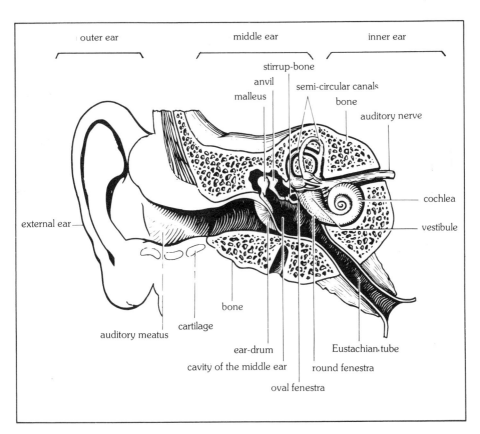

outer ear | middle ear | inner ear

stirrup-bone
anvil
malleus
semi-circular canals
bone
auditory nerve

cochlea

external ear

vestibule

auditory meatus
cartilage
bone
ear-drum
cavity of the middle ear
oval fenestra
round fenestra
Eustachian tube

What about animals' ears?

Fish have no external ears

The snail makes no sound and probably hears nothing either

A bird has no external ear, but its internal ear is very acute

The rabbit's ears turn towards the sound.

The ear is a sound receiver.

When sound meets an obstacle

Echoes

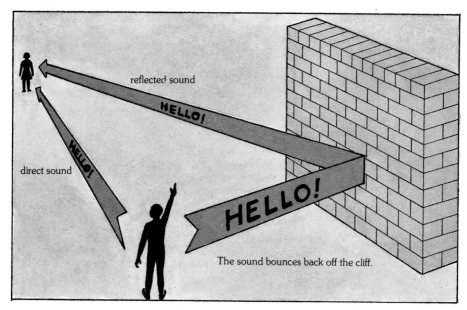

reflected sound

HELLO!

HELLO!

direct sound

HELLO!

The sound bounces back off the cliff.

When sound meets a solid object it is partially thrown back (or reflected, as we say). If you happen to be in line with the reflected sound, you hear an echo. Person No. 2 hears the same sound twice. Look at the diagram and explain why.

On the motorway

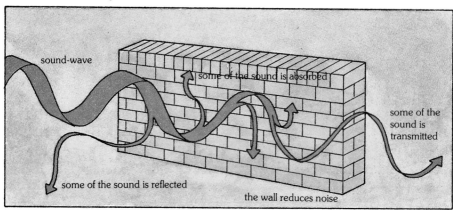

sound-wave

some of the sound is absorbed

some of the sound is transmitted

some of the sound is reflected

the wall reduces noise

Look at the drawing: you will see that the wall reflects and absorbs sound.

Something to do:
Look around the house for things which reduce noise:
double glazing, soft furnishings, curtains . . .
Make a list of things which absorb noise.

Sound can be reflected, absorbed or transmitted.

Ultrasound and infrasound

ultrasound	Vibrations which are too fast for our ears
audible sound	I can hear
infrasound	Vibrations which are too slow to be audible

the bat

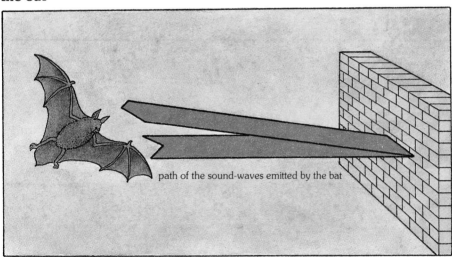

path of the sound-waves emitted by the bat

The bat finds its way about by means of sound. It emits ultrasonic squeaks, and the time taken for the echo to return gives it a very precise "picture" of its environment (radar works in a very similar way).

A dog's ear is more sensitive than our own, because it can hear ultrasounds. So we can summon a dog with an ultrasonic whistle without being able to hear the whistle ourselves.

Your dog can hear a car coming before you do (because cars emit both sounds and ultrasounds).

There are many vibrations in the air which our ears do not register.

Silence

Train your ear to hear very faint or distant sounds.

In reality, it is very difficult to achieve absolute silence here on earth. There are a multitude of vibrations in the air which may or may not be picked up by our ears.

You can hear the rapid vibrations of a fly's wings, but the slow beating of a butterfly's wings is inaudible.

We call the absence of audible sounds "silence". True silence is the complete absence of all sound.

A bit of history

In ancient times
Messages were passed from one person to another, and that was how information was transmitted.

The megaphone
A megaphone concentrates and directs the sound so that it can carry further. Make your own megaphone with a piece of card.

In the seventeenth century
The English physicist, Robert Hooke, succeeded in transmitting sound along a cord. His apparatus consisted of two open-ended cylinders, one end of which was covered with a thin skin and linked to the other cylinder with a piece of cord.

Something to do:
Try this experiment with two boxes and a piece of string.
Make a hole in the bottom of each box and join them together with a long piece of string with a knot on each end. Try to communicate . . .

To communicate you need to:

Emit ▶▶ ——————— Transmit ——————— ▶▶ Receive

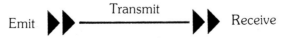

The use of space

Some theatres with almost perfect acoustics have been built. (Acoustics is a word used to describe the sound qualities of a theatre or concert hall.)

The theatre at Epidaurus (Greece, fourth century BC)

Have you ever moved house, and spoken or sung in an empty room? Did you notice any difference in the sound?

Sing or shout in a small room, under the shower, in a large hall. Compare what you hear.

Look for a photograph of an orchestra. The instruments are arranged in groups; where the players sit is important in producing musical harmony.

When you listen to a record or a cassette you can capture the atmosphere of a real concert by using a stereo player.

The Royal Albert Hall

Things to do:
Look up the definition of the word stereophonic (stereo)
Where do you put the two speakers?
Where must you sit in order to hear the best sound?

Emission, transmission

Let's see how we can transmit sound.
In 1680 a monk in the Abbey of Citeaux in France thought of a "quick and simple" way of speaking to people at a distance. He used a metal tube to "conduct the sounds".

Something to do:
Try using different sorts of tubes, both full and empty.
A medical use of sound – the stethoscope

Listening to a patient's chest

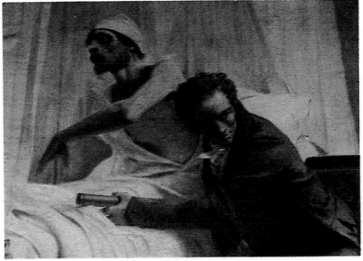

In the past

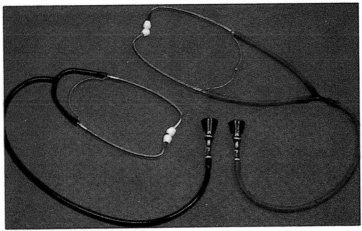

Nowadays

You can conduct sound over a short distance by using a tube.
But what do you do to communicate over a long distance?

23

Long-distance transmission: the telephone

A long journey

. . . A quiet voice . . . an abstract voice . . . a distant voice . . . and your loved one speaks your name. She is there, it is her voice you hear, but how far away it seems.

How unhappy I always feel at times like these, knowing that, without going on a long journey, it is impossible to see the one whose voice is so close to my ear. There is something very deceptive in being brought closer together . . .

Marcel Proust: *Time Remembered*

The telephone line

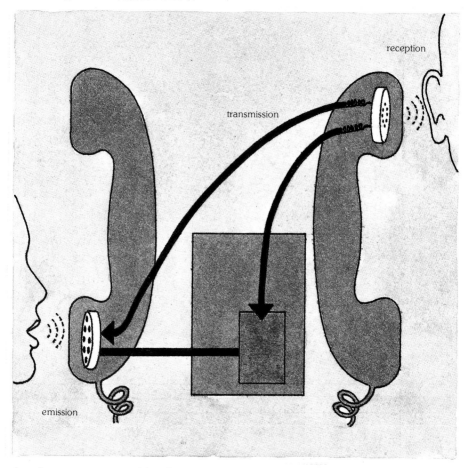

An electric current enables the message to travel over a long distance.

Leaving your message

"Spoken words fly away, only the written word remains . . ."

When you can't speak to somebody, you have to leave them a written message, unless of course they have an answering machine.

We must use a code to represent sound. In writing, we use the alphabet to reproduce the spoken word.

You write: barrow

You say: **(b) (a)**   **(r) (o)**

These are two phonemes which help us to reconstruct the spoken word.

Something to do:
Look for methods of writing other than your own.
To write music, we use a stave and notes.

What about other noises?

Writing does not always convey the sound very well.

From one tape to another

The barrel organ
The holes in the perforated band make the organ pipes vibrate. The organ works mechanically.

The cassette player
The music is recorded on magnetic tape.

From one disc to another
The phonograph was invented by an American named Thomas Edison. A needle traces the vibrations in the groove of a revolving disc, enabling the sound to be reproduced. His idea has been improved upon many times since then.

In each case you need something to record the sound on (1) and a player (2) to reproduce it.

Creating new sounds

A better knowledge of the way sound is made and the development of electronics, has led to equipment being made which can alter sounds or create echoes.

The sound-effects used by pop singers.

The study of sound has enabled us . . .
. . . to use the computer as a new musical instrument; to make synthetic music . . .
. . . and even to imitate the sound of the human voice.

Communication without words

Many years ago, a priest named Father Chappe, invented a visual code. He used three pieces of wood, painted black, which could be moved into different positions to represent different letters.

With people standing at regular intervals (equidistant from each other), using his equipment, a message could travel 1,000 kilometres (621 miles) in twenty minutes.

Morse code

The electric telegraph and the telegraphic alphabet were invented by the American, Samuel Morse, in 1837.

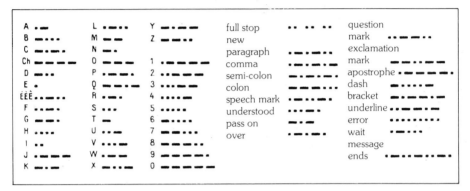

Other codes: Semaphore

Sailors use sign language to send messages from one boat to another.
There is a sign language for the deaf too.

Sight can supplement hearing.

Protect your ears and your vocal cords

If you smoke or if you sit in a smoke-filled room, after a while, the tars produced by burning tobacco settle on your vocal cords and damage them. Your voice becomes husky.

Good hearing is invaluable.
But your ears are very delicate.
   That is why we have to be sure that small children do not put anything in their ears.

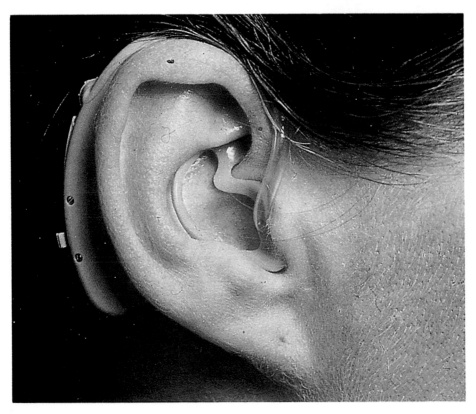

People who do not hear very well use a hearing-aid.

Look after your ears and your vocal cords.

Good sounds and bad noises

Sound can be:

— pleasant, like the crackling of a log, the murmur of a spring, or the song of a bird;
— uplifting, like music;
— frightening, like the rumble of thunder or the howling of a wild animal at night;
— throbbing, annoying and irritating, like those noises which assault our eardrums every day, and which may eventually do lasting damage.

A continuous noise is more tiring than an intense but fleeting one.

Noise affects your nerves, your sleep, your appetite.

It is the cause of many physical disorders and can lead to depression and insanity.

Don't forget, though, that sound gives you information about the world about you, and enables you to communicate with your friends.

Noise which is too loud

Listening for too long

Beware of excess noise.

Danger! Beware!

I firmly believe that one can be happy without causing unhappiness to others; that as well as the rights of the child, there are the rights of the parent: the right to rest, the right to silence at certain times, the right to work undisturbed.

Colette: *From my window*

Beware! Excess noise can be as harmful as drugs

Noise level measured in decibels		
	Threshold of pain	harmful noise
130	Gunfire	
120	Aircraft taking off	
110	Helicopter; pop group	
100	Factory machinery; pneumatic drill	
90	Domestic appliances; cars; motorcycles	workday noise
80	Heavy traffic; underground railways; trucks	
70	Typewriters; heated conversation	
60	Normal traffic	
50	Normal conversation	
40	Quiet room during the day	peace and quiet
30	Rustling of leaves in the undergrowth	
20	Quiet room at night	
10	A whisper a metre (a yard) away	
0	Threshold of audibility	

Did you know that there was a law against noise, and that anyone who breaks the law can be fined or sent to prison.
Find out about it.

Glossary

Audible: can be heard

Baritone: male voice between tenor and bass

Bass: Deep-sounding voice or instrument

Echo: Repetition of a sound, caused by sound-waves reflecting off some object

Height of a note: Its position in a scale going from low to high

Infrasound: Vibrations which are too slow to be audible

Microphone: Instrument which translates sound vibrations into electrical impulses

Oscilloscope: Instrument in which oscillations (vibrations) in electrical current produce a trace on a screen

Register (voice): Range of a singer's voice

Soprano: A singer with a high voice

Stereophonic: A realistic impression of sound achieved by using more than one microphone or speaker

Tenor: A high male voice

Tuning-fork: A small instrument which sounds the note "A". Used for tuning instruments

Ultrasound: Vibrations which are too rapid to be audible

Vocal cords: Membranes at the base of the throat which vibrate to produce the voice